D1313738

CANADA GOOSE

Amy-Jane Beer

Grolier
an imprint of

█ SCHOLASTIC

www.scholastic.com/librarypublishing

Published 2008 by Grolier
An imprint of Scholastic Library Publishing
Old Sherman Turnpike, Danbury,
Connecticut 06816

For The Brown Reference Group plc
Project Editor: Jolyon Goddard
Copy-editors: Lesley Ellis, Lisa Hughes,
    Wendy Horobin
Picture Researcher: Clare Newman
Designers: Jeni Child, Lynne Ross,
    Sarah Williams
Managing Editor: Bridget Giles

Volume ISBN-13: 978-0-7172-6251-9
Volume ISBN-10: 0-7172-6251-0

**Library of Congress
Cataloging-in-Publication Data**

Nature's children. Set 2.
    p. cm.
    Includes bibliographical references and
    index.
    ISBN-13: 978-0-7172-8081-0
    ISBN-10: 0-7172-8081-0
    1. Animals--Encyclopedias, Juvenile. I.
    Grolier (Firm)
    QL49.N383 2007
    590--dc22
                        2007026928

Printed and bound in China

PICTURE CREDITS

Front Cover: **Shutterstock**: Paul Williams.

Back Cover: **Shutterstock**: Linda Bucklin,
Jarvis Gray, David P. Lewis, The Final Image.

Alamy: John E. Marriott 34; **Ardea**: Francois
Gohier 29; **Corbis**: James L. Amos 18; **FLPA**:
David Hosking 45; **Nature PL**: T. J. Rich 41;
Photolibrary.com: Berndt-Joel
Gunnarsson 4; **Photos.com**: 10, 38, 46;
Shutterstock: Don Blais 5, Bryan Eastham
14, Tim Elliott 42, Jarvis Gray 30, Cindy
Haggerty 9, Per-Anders Jansson 21, Denise
Kappa 26–27, Jason Kasumovic 22, Robert
Kelsey 2–3, Nicole Kessel 6, 33, Svetlana
Lanna 13, Jeff Thrower 37; **Still Pictures**:
Diane Sharpiro 17.

Contents

FACT FILE: Canada Goose

Class	Aves (birds)
Order	Anseriformes
Family	Ducks, geese, and swans (Anatidae)
Genus	*Branta*
Species	*Branta canadensis*
World distribution	Originally from North America, but now widespread in Europe, too, after being taken there by humans
Habitat	Lakes, ponds, slow-flowing rivers, marshes, and grasslands close to freshwater
Distinctive physical characteristics	Brown body plumage, pale chest, black head and neck with bright white patch running from cheek to cheek under the throat
Habits	Forms large flocks, communicates using calls and body language, pairs for life, migrates south for winter
Diet	Grass, water plants, seeds, grain, and insects

Introduction

Canada geese may be the most familiar birds in all of North America. They range from the far north to the deep south, from the Arctic to the Gulf Coast. These large waterbirds can be heard honking in the country and in cities. They gather in parks, on golf courses, on beaches, and even in backyards. If you see one in your yard, don't get too close. Their large wings are also used as weapons. So watch out!

A Canada goose takes a rest.

Nearly everyone recognizes the black head, white chin, and long black neck of the Canada goose.

Canada's Finest

Canada is famous for many things—maple syrup, great mountains, and forests. Canada is also famous for its wonderful wildlife, including eagles, moose, and grizzly bears. But it might be most well known for the Canada goose. There are different types of Canada geese. They all have similar **plumage**, or feathers, but they vary in shape and size. The biggest females weigh around 17 pounds (8 kg). That's as much some human toddlers.

Not all Canada geese live in Canada. Some live in the United States. Many live in Europe, too. They were taken there by humans around 300 years ago, and they have adapted well to their new home.

Duck, Duck, Goose!

Geese are related to other waterbirds, such as ducks and swans. If you look carefully you can see a family likeness. They all have a large, chunky body, a long neck, and powerful wings. The legs are short and they have big webbed feet. Most Canada geese also have a large beak.

Geese, ducks, and swans like to live in similar places; they are all waterbirds. These birds are also known as waterfowl. "**Fowl**" is another word for bird. Unlike birds that nest in trees, all ducks, swans, and geese build their nests on the ground.

Canada geese are waterbirds and are related to ducks and swans.

A flock of Canada geese gathers beside a lake.

Earth, Air, and Water

Canada geese seem to have the best of three worlds. They are just as at home on water and in the air as they are walking around on land. They often seem to go wherever they please. A large **flock** of Canada geese has little to fear from **predators**. There are usually one or two birds standing guard at all times. At the first sign of danger the guards give a loud honk or cackle. Not many predators can follow the geese into water, and even fewer can fly, so the geese nearly always make a safe escape.

Feather Facts

The outer feathers on a Canada goose's body are smooth, flat, and stiff. The largest feathers are on the wings and tail. They give each wing its special shape, which allows the bird to fly. Each feather is shaped like a long leaf, with a stalk in the center and several tiny side branches or "combs" that zip together to form a **plume**.

The outer feathers are a little greasy. Using its beak, the goose collects oil from a gland under its tail. It then spreads the oil onto all its feathers to make them waterproof. The goose only has to shake its feathers and all the water runs off in little droplets. The waterproofing oil also prevents the skin and under feathers from getting wet.

Spreading out
its wing feathers,
a Canada goose
lands on water.

13

Beneath the outer feathers lies a layer of fluffy down feathers. These feathers trap air and keep the goose warm at all times.

14

Deep Down

Geese have two kinds of feathers. The outer feathers and the under feathers. The under feathers are very small and fluffy. They are called **down**. Their job is to keep the goose warm. They do that by trapping air next to the goose's skin. The air stays nice and warm and dry because it is protected from the wind and wet by the outer feathers. A goose's two sets of feathers are a little like wearing a really thick, fluffy sweater under a waterproof coat. A goose stays warm even when it swims in very cold water. Goose down is so warm that humans use it, too, to fill the linings of coats and quilts, for example.

Bath Time

Canada geese spend a lot of time looking after their feathers. Baby geese learn to wash and care for their feathers from a very early age. Bath time can look more like playtime—the geese really seem to enjoy splashing around. Flapping their wings allows water to run through their feathers and carrying away all the dust and dirt. Sometimes the geese turn somersaults in the water to make sure all the feathers on their back get rinsed really well.

When the feathers are clean, it's time to make sure they are neat. The goose uses its beak as a comb to straighten its feathers. It then waterproofs them with oil.

Using its beak as a comb, this Canada goose cleans and waterproofs its feathers.

With their wings
flapping wildly,
a flock of Canada
geese takes off.

18

Taking to the Air

Canada geese are bigger and heavier than most other flying birds. These large fowl are the jumbo jets of the bird world. In fact, Canada geese are great fliers. They can travel for hours at speeds of up to 40 miles (65 km) an hour.

The hardest part of flying is taking off. When a goose wants to fly, it starts by running with its wings spread. If you have ever tried to fly a kite, you'll know that a bit of speed over the ground helps get it into the air. Geese can also take off from water by half paddling and half running, with their feet slapping the surface.

Flappy Feet

Geese have short legs covered with scaly skin.
The scales protect the geese from scrapes and
scratches. The legs are the only part of the body
not covered with feathers, so they sometimes get
cold. That is one reason geese often stand on
one leg—the other one is tucked away, nice and
warm, in its feathers.

Goose feet are really big. They are triangular,
with four long toes joined by a web of skin. The
webbing turns the feet into really great paddles,
much like the flippers worn by divers. The toes
also have sturdy claws, which help the goose
grip on slippery mud.

Sound asleep, a Canada
goose balances on one leg.

The large eyes on either side of a goose's head give it excellent vision.

Super Senses

Canada geese have bright, beady eyes and can see well. They need sharp eyes to watch for predators, such as foxes, and to help them find their way when they are flying.

You can't see a goose's ears, but they are there, hidden under the feathers on the sides of the head. Geese can hear extremely well. Good hearing helps them sense danger even in darkness. They can also hear other geese coming from miles away.

A famous story from ancient Rome tells how geese saved the city by raising the alarm when an army of Barbarians tried to creep in. The geese in the story weren't Canada geese, but no doubt they would have done just as good a job. Many people still keep "guard geese" to warn them of trespassers!

Eat Your Greens

Geese eat mainly plants, especially grass, water weeds, and grains. But they are not strict vegetarians. They also enjoy insects, spiders, water lice, and little shrimps they find among the plants.

When geese are feeding on water plants, they tip themselves upside down in the water. They use their long neck to reach down to the bottom to find food. If the water is dark or cloudy, the geese can feel their way around with their beak. The edge of the beak has little spikes like the teeth of a comb. These spikes allow the water to drain out of the beak.

Geese do not have real teeth like humans, so they have to swallow their food without chewing it. The food gets mashed up in a part of the stomach called the **gizzard**.

Honk, Honk!

Geese can be noisy animals. They make a variety of sounds, including a loud honking sound and a warning hiss. The baby geese, called **goslings**, make a cheeping sound when they are very young.

Geese use honking as a way of keeping in touch with the rest of the flock. They often honk when they are flying in formation and can't see one another. A quick honk lets the bird in front know everyone else is still there!

If you walk too close to a flock of geese, especially when there are young around, the adults will watch you closely and make a loud hissing sound with their beak open. Sometimes they will walk toward you with their wings spread open. That makes them look really big. This sign clearly means "Go away"! The best thing to do is to back off to show you mean them no harm.

Adult geese and
their young enjoy
a grassy meal
beside a lake.

The Flying V

Geese and some other birds nearly always fly in formation. Sometimes you'll see them in a long diagonal line. But usually they form a great big "V" shape in the sky. The V is called a **skein** (SKANE). The reason geese fly like that is so they can save energy. Flying is hard work, especially if the birds are flying into strong wind. By positioning itself behind and just to the side of another bird, flying becomes much easier for the goose. The air rushing off the wings of the bird in front helps lift the one behind.

The lead bird does not get any extra help. Not surprisingly, every few minutes the bird at the front of the "V" gets too tired to continue. It then drops back to let another bird take the lead.

A flock of geese flies in formation, one tucked just behind the other.

29

A pair of Canada geese
flies south to escape
the cold winter.

Incredible Journey

Winter in Canada and the northern United States can be tough, especially in an area called the **tundra**. There it's very cold and the ground is often covered with thick snow. In addition, the rivers, marshes, and lakes freeze over. That all makes it really hard for Canada geese to find enough to eat. So, very sensibly, they leave! Every fall, the geese gather in great big flocks and head south. They fly all the way to the Gulf of Mexico. This **annual** trip takes several weeks to complete.

Flocks of geese from different parts of North America travel south using regular routes called **flyways**. There are four main flyways. Two flyways are **coastal**—one follows the Atlantic coast and the other follows the Pacific coast. The third flyway follows the Mississippi River, while the fourth flyway winds down through the central and midwestern states.

Smart Moves

Once a goose has made its first long journey south, it always remembers the route. It will then travel the same way every time. There are always several geese in the flock that have made the trip before and can lead the way. Each goose has a built-in compass, so it knows which way is south, even in pitch darkness or dense fog. The geese also use the position of the Sun and the stars to get their bearings. They follow landmarks, such as rivers, mountain ranges, and coastlines, too. The geese stop to rest and feed at the same places every year on their journey south.

Geese often use landmarks, such as mountain ranges, to find their way south.

33

Once they have
chosen a partner,
Canada geese
pair up for life.

Goose and Gander

A male goose is called a **gander** and a female goose is called…well, a goose. Young geese are ready to pair up when they are two or three years old. Young ganders spend a few days watching the females to see which one they like best. Sometimes ganders will fight over their favorite goose. If the goose is interested, she will allow the gander to come close. She then copies his movements. The pair face each other and bob their heads, honking loudly. If she is not interested, she will keep moving away, hissing at the gander until he gets the message! Once a goose and a gander have paired up, they stay together for life.

Building a Nest

Spring is nesting time. Pairs of geese begin looking for a good nest site as soon as they arrive back from their winter **migration**. Like all geese, Canada geese nest on the ground, close to water. Sometimes they have to fight other pairs of geese for a really good site. The strongest pair drives the others away, with their necks stretched out low, hissing, and flapping their wings. Then they get to work on the nest. First they collect a heap of grass, reeds, and twigs. Then the female goose makes a hollow in the top of the heap and lines it with soft feathers plucked from her chest.

A Canada goose sits atop a large nest, keeping her eggs warm and safe from predators.

Five large, creamy eggs nestle among the feathers and grass of a goose's nest.

Precious Eggs

After **mating**, a female goose lays a cream-colored egg every one or two days for about a week. She plucks more feathers from her chest until there is a bare patch of skin there. When she settles on the nest, this patch of skin is pressed against the eggs. The eggs are then warmed by the mother goose's body heat. Every so often, she turns over the eggs with her beak so that they stay warm all over. Inside the eggs, the goslings are growing bigger and bigger by the day.

Hello Mother!

While her mate watches over her, the mother goose sits on her eggs for about a month. That is how long it takes for the goslings to develop. When it is time to hatch, a gosling uses a little peg on the top of its beak called an egg tooth to peck a hole in the eggshell. Often, the gosling starts cheeping as soon as the shell is cracked. After a few minutes of hard work, pushing with its feet and wings, the gosling forces the eggshell apart and tumbles out into the world.

Baby geese are born with an instinct to follow the first thing they see after they hatch. Usually that is their mother. A very special bond forms between the goose and her babies in the first few minutes of their life. This bond is called **imprinting**. If the first thing the baby goose sees is another animal or a human, it will choose to follow that instead.

Small and fluffy,
a day-old gosling
sits safely in its nest.

Soon after hatching, the goslings are happily bobbing about on water.

Follow the Leader

When goslings first hatch, they are covered in soggy feathers. It takes just a few minutes for the babies to dry out into fluffy, yellow powder puffs. As soon as all her eggs have hatched, the mother goose leads the goslings to the water. The babies scurry after their mother as fast as their legs will carry them, cheeping all the while. They plop into the water and start swimming right away. They learn to feed by copying their mother.

It is a dangerous time for the goslings. On land, there are predators, such as cats, foxes, and snakes, that might eat them. On the water, the baby geese might be grabbed by a heron or a big fish, such as a pike. But the goslings grow fast and at just seven weeks old, they are big and strong enough to fly.

Earthbound

When a bird's feathers become worn, they fall off, or **molt**. They are replaced by new feathers, which grow from the skin. Some birds replace their flight feathers one at a time. In this way, they can always manage to fly. But ducks and geese molt their flight feathers all at once. Then they grow a whole new set of feathers. Bird experts call this type of molt an **eclipse**. It means that these birds cannot fly for a few weeks while their new feathers grow.

Eclipse is a tricky time for geese. Not being able to fly makes it harder to escape predators. But these are smart birds. They know that while they cannot fly, they can swim as well as ever. They spend nearly all of their time out in the middle of lakes, where they are out of the reach of hungry hunters.

While they grow new flight feathers, these geese stay in the middle of the lake, safe from predators.

A Canada goose
swims in an
English lake.

Traveling Abroad

Canada geese were first taken to Europe more than 300 years ago. Rich Englishmen thought the geese would look good swimming on the lakes at their great country houses. So, the birds were taken over from North America in ships and set free. The English countryside is perfect for Canada geese. The summer weather is warm and there are plenty of fresh green plants to eat. Also, the winter weather is not as cold as it is in Canada, so the geese do not even need to fly south in winter. What a life!

These days there are thousands of Canada geese in Great Britain—they are more common than any other goose. Wild Canada geese also live in Scandinavia and in New Zealand.

Living with Geese

Everyone knows a good goose story. From the tales and nursery rhymes of Mother Goose to the legend of the goose that laid golden eggs, the stories are countless.

People have been interested in geese for thousands of years. To begin with, geese were seen mainly as food. But they had many other uses, too. Their warm down was used to make clothing and quilts, their feathers made the quill pens that people once used to write with, and their fat was used to make ointments and even candles. Geese were such a big part of everyday life long ago that many sayings about them are still used today. We say "a wild goose chase" to mean a waste of time. A "goose egg" in sports is bad news—it means a score of zero.

Words to Know

Annual   Once a year.

Coastal   By the sea.

Down   The small, soft under feathers that keep a goose warm.

Eclipse   Annual molt, when geese and ducks lose their worn-out flight feathers and cannot fly until new ones grow.

Flock   A group of geese.

Flyways   Migration routes in the sky.

Fowl   Birds that humans farm or hunt for food, such as geese and chickens.

Gander   A male goose.

Gizzard   The part of a goose's stomach that grinds up food.

Goslings	Baby geese.
Imprinting	The way goslings fix on the first moving thing they see when they hatch, usually their mother.
Mating	Coming together to produce young.
Migration	A long journey, usually a round trip taken at the same time each year.
Molt	To shed old feathers and replace them with new ones.
Plumage	A bird's feathers.
Plume	The soft part of a feather.
Predators	Animals that hunt other animals.
Skein	The V-shape formation of flying geese.
Tundra	The treeless landscape of the far north, into the Arctic Circle.

Find Out More

Books

Burnie, D. *The Concise Animal Encyclopedia*. Boston, Massachusetts: Kingfisher/Houghton Mifflin, 2003.

Choiniere, J. and C. Mowbray Golding. *What's That Bird?* North Adams, Massachusetts: Storey Publishing, 2005.

Web sites

All About Birds
www.birds.cornell.edu/AllAboutBirds/BirdGuide/Canada_Goose.html
Detailed information about Canada geese.

Kidzone—Canada Geese
www.kidzone.ws/animals/birds/canada-goose.htm
Facts about Canadian geese, with a picture to print and color in, plus worksheets.

Index